KT-484-778

Larrrd!
GOLF SALE
DANDY BOOK ENTRANCE
NO SHOES
SCRIPT IDEAS
Hufff!

Sign here, please!
THIS BOOK BELONGS TO.....

Right! We need a security thumbprint on this screen!
Look in my eye for eyeball recognition - good.
DNA identification now - a saliva sample is required - SPIT!
Show us your belly!
Now you put your left foot in...
...INOUTINOUTSHAKEITALLABOUTDOTHEHOKEY...
Silly guard had a sneak peek inside - he's suffering a fun overload!
There's nothing to see here - move along to the rest of the Dandy Book!
Giggle!

KORKY THE CAT
Who are you?
I'm Korky.
MILK
Hey! You can talk! But aren't you a cat?
So can you, but I don't go on about it – and yes – I happen to be a cat.
How come you don't walk on all fours like a cat?
This just happens to be the way I walk.
Ah! That's what cats do – have a bowl of milk!
Bowl of MILK? You're having a laugh, aren't you?
MILK
I'm having a bowl of WheatyFlakes – milk's too wet without cereal!
WHEATYFLAKES
You don't even eat like a real cat!
WHEATYFLAKES
I chew! Chomp! I swallow! Gulp! What other way to eat is there?

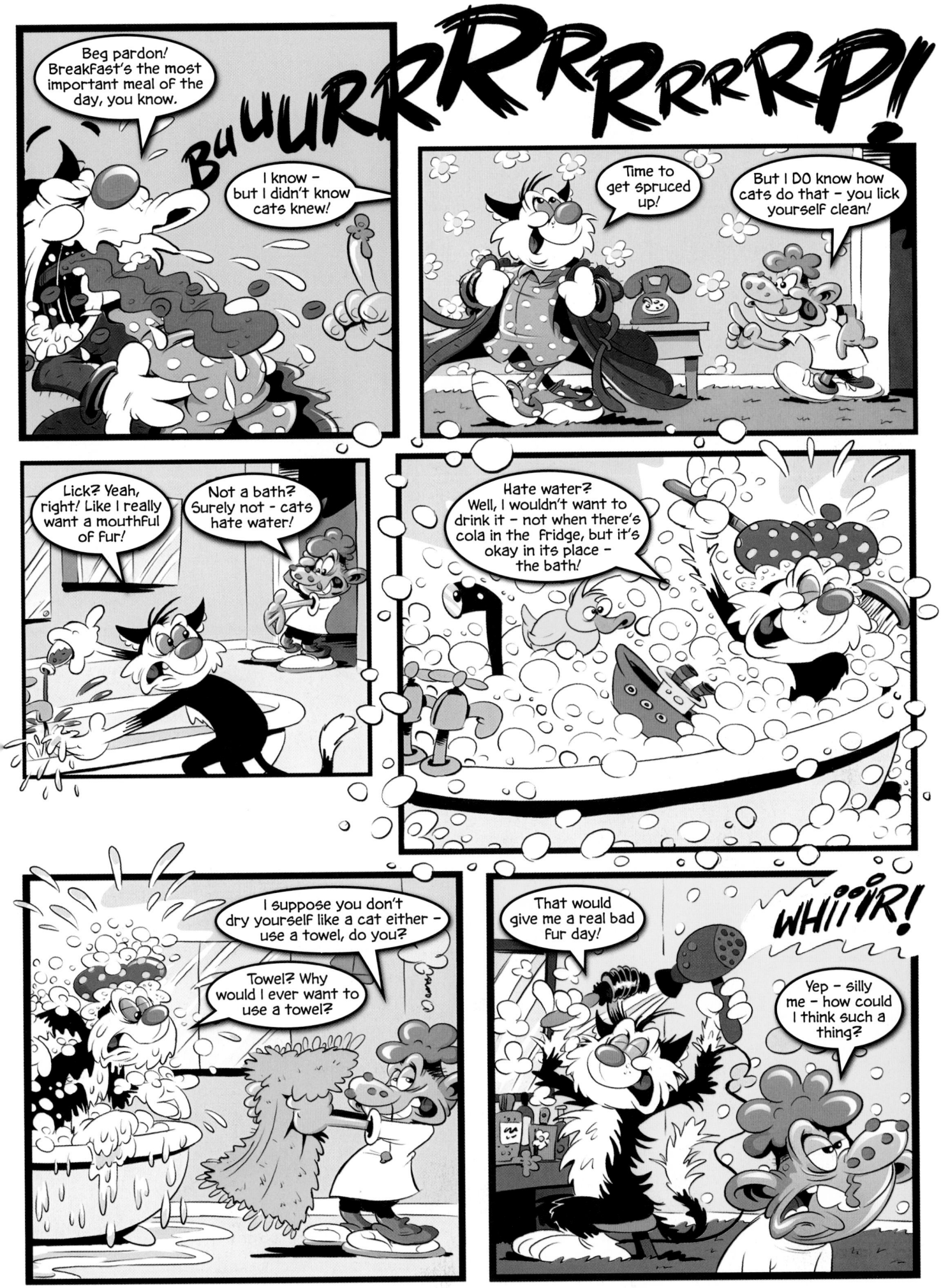
Beg pardon! Breakfast's the most important meal of the day, you know.
BuUURRRRRRRRP!
I know – but I didn't know cats knew!
Time to get spruced up!
But I DO know how cats do that – you lick yourself clean!
Lick? Yeah, right! Like I really want a mouthful of fur!
Not a bath? Surely not – cats hate water!
Hate water? Well, I wouldn't want to drink it – not when there's cola in the fridge, but it's okay in its place – the bath!
I suppose you don't dry yourself like a cat either – use a towel, do you?
Towel? Why would I ever want to use a towel?
That would give me a real bad fur day!
WHIIIR!
Yep – silly me – how could I think such a thing?

Not too shabby, if I say so myself – time to go!
Going to walk round your territory, are you?
Walk? You're funny – you should be in comics – not The Dandy though – you're not THAT funny!
Aw, c'mon! Cats do NOT drive cars!
Snigger! Not very well anyway! Giggle! You don't do anything like a real cat!
CRUMP!
POLICE
POLICE
Who did it? Who pranged my motor? Who?
I saw it all, officer! I'm a witness! Me! I saw it!
POLICE

It was HIM!
Who? Him?
He can't drive – he's a cute, little pussycat – which only leaves...
B-B-But it WAS! It WAS him, I tell you!
OF course I can behave like a real cat – WHEN I WANT TO!
It was HIM! I'm telling you – I wasn't driving – honest!
Don't tell me, pal – tell it to the judge!

It's nice, quiet and peaceful with Blinky out of the house.
YESSSSS! I'VE DONE IT!
SPLART!!!
S-So have I!
What have you done - and, more importantly, why?
I've just broken my record for flying my kite, Mother.
SQUELCH
I'm good at it too - it's been up there for ages!
That's because it's stuck - up a tree!
Stuck? How will I get it down?
Oh, use your head for once, Blinky!
Knock it down, eh? Got it! Brilliant plan, Mother!
CHARGE!
SMACK!
Groan! Using your head doesn't half make it sore...

BOK! BOK! BOK! BOK! BOK!
...V-VERY sore!
I suppose a caring mum would lend a hand at this point!
Get ready to grab your kite, Blinky.
Now!
Got it!
Giggle! I shouldn't laugh really! I shouldn't have let the string go either!
TWANG!
Okay! Where's HERE - and how did I get up it?
Your Christmas Tree's a bit scraggy, isn't it? The Fairy on top's seen better days as well, Missus!
Spare me!
NICK BRENNAN

HISTORICAL MEERKATS
CAESAR
BRITAIN Welcomes careful Drivers
SPLOSH!
DO NOT STAUDUS IN THE WOAD

BANANAMAN
ORIGINS
This is Little Eric's Mum!
This is Little Eric – or it will be soon...
...very, VERY soon!
HOSPITAL
AMBULANCE
AMBULANCE
SCREECH!
Very, VERY soon...
Don't know what all the fuss was about – everyone said I'd be screaming...
...but it was a dawdle – not a whimper passed my lips!
Here's your baby – it's a little...

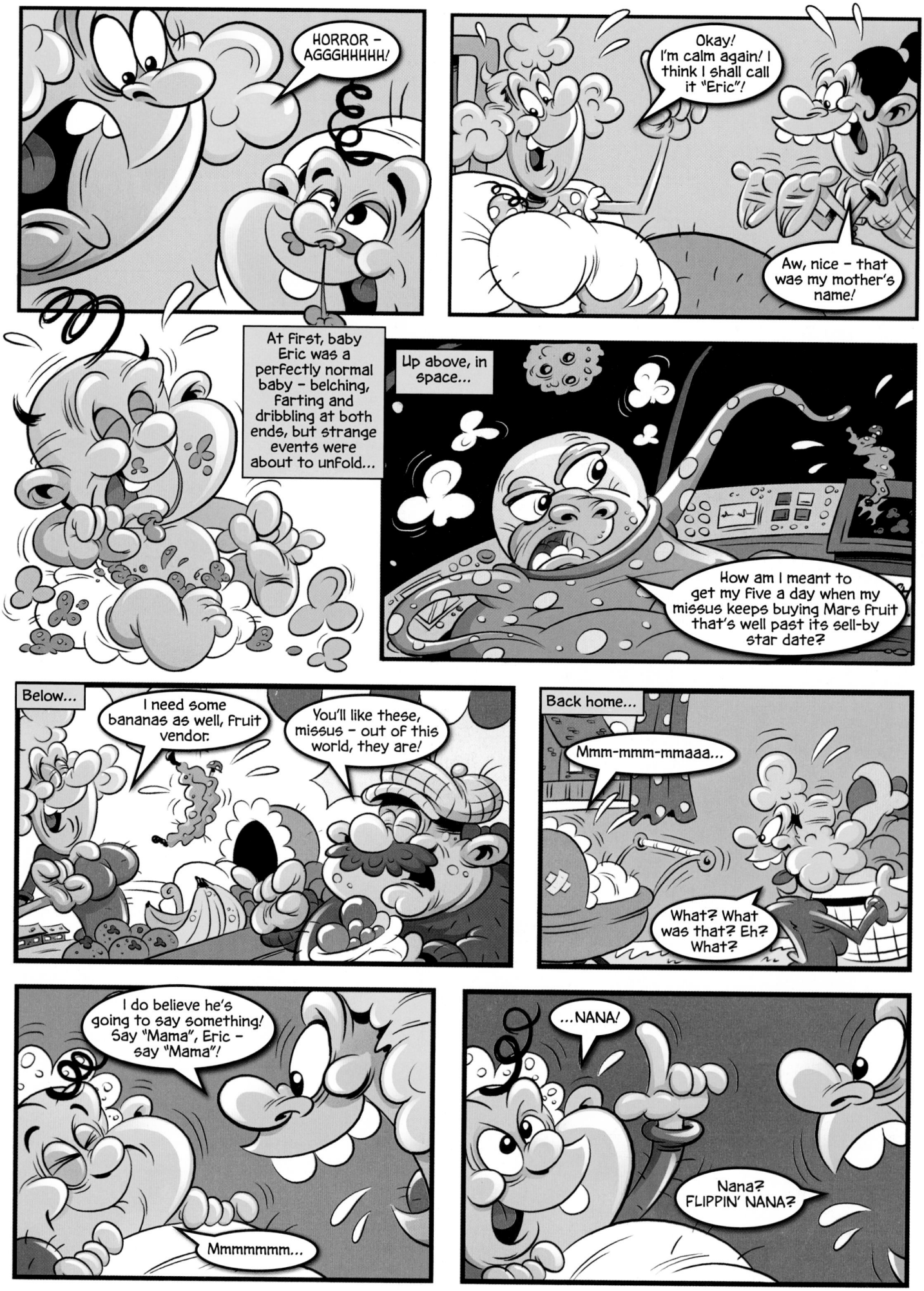
HORROR – AGGGHHHHH!
Okay! I'm calm again! I think I shall call it "Eric"!
Aw, nice – that was my mother's name!
At first, baby Eric was a perfectly normal baby – belching, farting and dribbling at both ends, but strange events were about to unfold...
Up above, in space...
How am I meant to get my five a day when my missus keeps buying Mars fruit that's well past its sell-by star date?
Below...
I need some bananas as well, fruit vendor.
You'll like these, missus – out of this world, they are!
Back home...
Mmm-mmm-mmaaa...
What? What was that? Eh? What?
I do believe he's going to say something! Say "Mama", Eric – say "Mama"!
Mmmmmmm...
...NANA!
Nana? FLIPPIN' NANA?

Here! Have your banana! See if I care that you prefer 'nanas to your Mama! Am I bothered? Um – no!
FA-ZAAM!
Oh, bad move, Eric's mum! That was no ordinary banana! No – that's been bombarded with Grammar – er – Grandma – er – Gammon – er – some kind of ray! Who knows what effect it will have on little Eric? Well, anybody who has read The Dandy will know – and the guy who wrote this – he'll know! Okay, EVERYBODY will know – except Beano readers – they won't know, because we won't tell them!
Good gracious! Who would have thought it? When little Eric eats a banana, he becomes a Bananaman!
SHHH! DON'T TELL THE BEANO READERS!
Readers' voices
Wah! Sob! Howl! Wail! Boo-hoo!
Eek!

Now see what you did! There, there – the nasty readers won't ever do that again, Diddums!
BURRRRRRRRRRP!
Gurgle! Goo!
Never mind the readers – DON'T YOU EVER DO THAT AGAIN – NEVER EVER!
CHRIS McCHIE

BULLY BEEF and CHIPS
PIZZA
OPEN
Yum-yum! Pizza!
Sounds good to me – let's see if it tastes good as well! I could do with a bite!
Hey! Let me have it!
You can have some of it – here's the box!
Give me my lunch, you ruffian!
Okay – open wide!
My own special recipe – pizza with extra iron! Cackle!
Glumph!
Spit!
YAROO!
Argh! This w-wasn't the kind of "bite" I had in m-mind!
Looks as if these sewer rats want a "PIZZA" you, Beefy! Snigger!

CORPORAL CLOTT
Corporal Cott is on the firing range...
Good grief!
POW
PING
POP
PING
POP POW
Corporal Clott! That has to be the worst shooting I have ever seen!!!
Get me that target!
Sir! Yes, sir!
I can't believe it! How did you manage to hit the target so often?
It's easier if you put all the holes in the target before you put it all the way back there!
WHAT!?!
Oops! Did I say that out loud?
As a punishment, Colonel Grumbly sends Corporal Clott on a ten mile hike...
Mutter, grumble, stupid boy...
Huff
Puff
...mutter, makes my life a, mutter... grumble...
Wish I'd never set eyes on... mutter...
Causes more trouble than the bloomin' enemy!
Wha! Hoo!

10 miles later...
Thanks for the ride, Grandad.
Glad to help.
BASE ENTRANCE
Hi there, Mister Grumbly, I'm back. Did you miss me?
That's Colonel Grumbly, lad.
Strange. He's not even sweating. I suppose he must be fitter than I thought.
Excuse me, Colonel Grumbly. We have an elderly gentleman at the front gate on a mobility scooter...
..he says Corporal Clott left his chocolate in his scooter when he gave him a lift.
Nigel Auchterlounie
Shall I give it to him?
NO! I'LL GIVE IT TO HIM!!!
Corporal Clott!!! Your grandad handed in your chocolate bar! You left it when he gave you a lift!!!
Oh goody!
Oh, no. Wait a minute.
Finish that chocolate, Clott. You'll need the energy.
I need a lift myself!
Come on, Clott. Only 8 more miles!
What? Colonel Grumbly has to win sometimes!

Desperate DAN
I'm Desperate Dan, the very bored man.
I wonder what it feels like to be small?
I wonder what it feels like to be VERY small?
I wonder where my nephew, Dan, is?
Erk! I wonder how I got to be so tall?
Dan! I might have guessed – you're always under my feet!
Can't help it, Aunt Aggie – I'm bored!
DAN'S U.S. TOUR
PART ONE
NIGEL PARKINSON.
R.T.W.

Take a holiday, why don't you? I could use the break!
A holiday? Great idea – I'll do a camping holiday!
I'll need some tinned grub...
...some milk, cheese, bacon and stuff...
...and a camp bed!
Mustn't forget a seat for sitting round the old campfire at night!
How d-did I get down here?
Hey! You're not helping, Aunt Aggie – why are you always under my feet?
Eh?

Under HIS Feet? Hey!
I'll need a lamp to read my Dandy at night - this'll do.
And I'll need the kitchen sink - in case there's no water nearby.
NO! NOT THE SINK!
Why not? You don't need it - there's plenty water in here!
WHAT?!?

Er – I'll just go then – shall I? I'll send a postcard.
Out! Out! OUT!

What a grouch! I would never have touched the sink if I'd known she didn't like sharing!

But I won't let it spoil my holiday.
CACTUSVILL

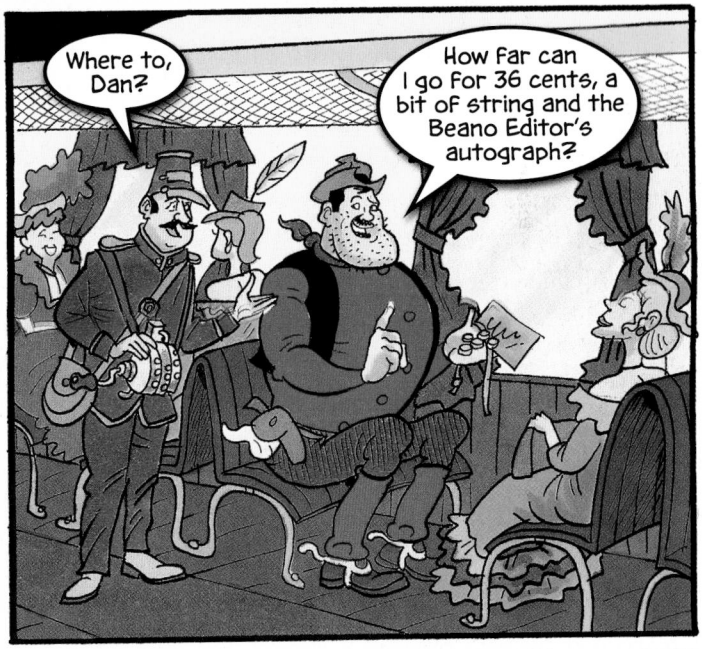
Where to, Dan?
How far can I go for 36 cents, a bit of string and the Beano Editor's autograph?

So that'll be not very far then?

Sigh! It looks like I'm walking, Folks!
See what happens in Part 2 later!

Fiddle O'Diddle
Where's Fiddle off to? To his gold, no doubt!
Take no notice of me, Fiddle, just keep going.
If you're after me gold, Muldoon, you might as well give up.
I'm visiting my wee pals, the Dancing Rocks of Sham.
The who?
No, not them. Just the Dancing Rocks of Sham!
Forget me loot, as I toot on me flute!

'Tis amazing!
NIK HOLMES
With these rocks I could make a fortune on 'Rathprune's Got Talent!'
Toot.
Gotcha!
Ah, if it isn't Tiny, come for a wee jig!
Tiny?
CRUNCH
Help?

Beryl the Peril
I'll show old Beaky – that's my dad by the way! I'll run away with the circus! That'll teach him to make me clean my room TWICE in a year!
Run aways Entrance
Trades mans Entrance
That'll be the door for me thataway!
Hey! Who runs this joint?
The guy in the top hat – now let go of my wire!
SHRIEK!
Hoi, top hat guy – we need to talk!
TWANG
No, I think you'll find that we don't need to talk!
Yes, we do, mate! I'm Beryl the Periloni and I'm your new star attraction!
Oh, yes? And what exactly can you do? Can you tame lions?
Can I? Can I tame lions? Watch this!
No! She didn't just do what I thought she did, did she?
THWAX
Y-You knocked him out!
You asked if I could tame lions – well, this one looks pretty tame to me!

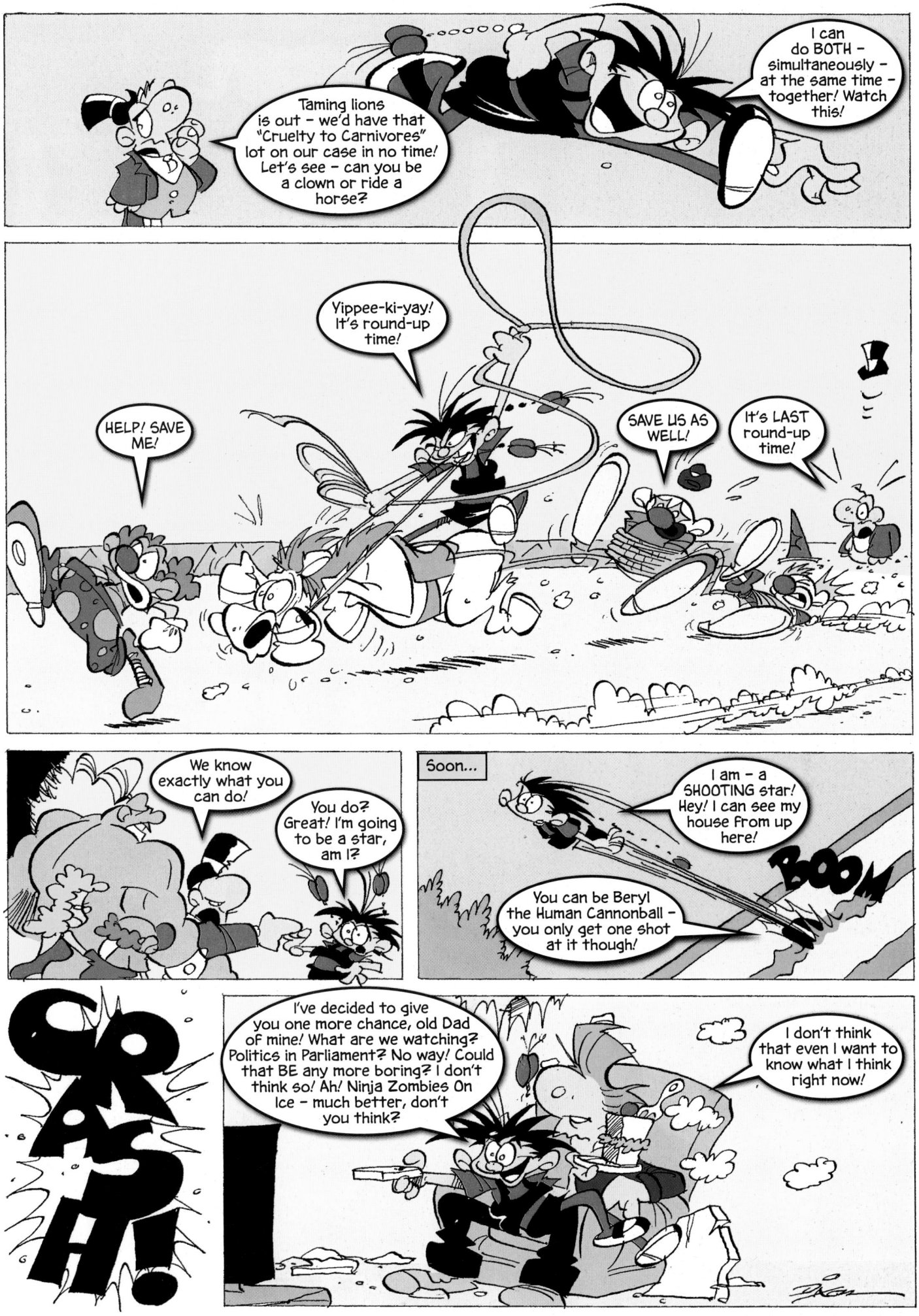
Taming lions is out – we'd have that "Cruelty to Carnivores" lot on our case in no time! Let's see – can you be a clown or ride a horse?
I can do BOTH – simultaneously – at the same time – together! Watch this!
Yippee-ki-yay! It's round-up time!
HELP! SAVE ME!
SAVE US AS WELL!
It's LAST round-up time!
We know exactly what you can do!
You do? Great! I'm going to be a star, am I?
Soon...
I am – a SHOOTING star! Hey! I can see my house from up here!
BOOM
You can be Beryl the Human Cannonball – you only get one shot at it though!
CRASH!
I've decided to give you one more chance, old Dad of mine! What are we watching? Politics in Parliament? No way! Could that BE any more boring? I don't think so! Ah! Ninja Zombies On Ice – much better, don't you think?
I don't think that even I want to know what I think right now!

George vs Dragon
There's one thing us dragons like more than a gentle day's fishing...
NO fishing
Bob!
Dip!
...and that's CATCHING a fish! And one thing us dragons like more than catching a fish...
SPLISH!
Uh-oh! Look who it is!
...is COOKING and EATING a fish! PUUUUFF!
Fry!
Tippy toe!
Of course, a fish needs KETCHUP - I'll just shake this to make it flow easier!
Shake! Shake! Shake!
Hee-hee...
Sneak!
HA! Prepare to be KEBABBED, fiend!
Sigh.
WHOOOOOSH!
LEAP!
Fry!
Burn!
Ha-HAH! I thought you'd do that, but thanks to my new FIREPROOF armour from Honest Erthelstan, I'm SAFE!
Hmm... what was it I did to that ketchup?

Ah, yes – I gave it a good shake to loosen it!
WHOOSH!
CLANG!
C-C-cease!

Brrrr!
Chilly? Can't have you getting cold...
Shiver!
Knobbly knees knocking!

Allow me to warm you up!
YAAARGH! Too warm!
Run!
FWOOOMPH!

Later...
Aw, not you again? I take it that new armour is also fireproof, huh?
Right first time, fish-face!

And it's no use shaking me – this armour is SHAKEPROOF, as well!
I was just going to do what I usually do next with a bottle of ketchup...
RAZZ!
Smug!

...And give it a good WHACK!
SMACK!
WHOOSH!
ooofyah!
Yowch!
Face-Mangling THUD!!

And so...
Honest Erthelstan
Bespoke armour dealer
MUD PIES
MUD CAKES
MUD BUNS
Got any Sauce-proof armour?
FANTON

HISTORICAL
MEERKATS
CLEOPATRA
HEAVE

WINKER WATSON
in
"Monkey Trouble"
Check this out, Winker – it's Mr Creep's driving licence!
And see where he was born, Trotty – Crawley!
So that makes him a CREEPY CRAWLEY! Hee-hee!
I heard that, Watson! Take a thousand lines – "I must not mock my superiors!"
Groan!
Pay attention, rabble! The prize for the School Of The Year Contest is a month at Swot Camp!
No-o-o! The EVIL place!
The school inspectors will be visiting Greytowers tomorrow – so be on your best behaviour – got it?
Yeah – right!

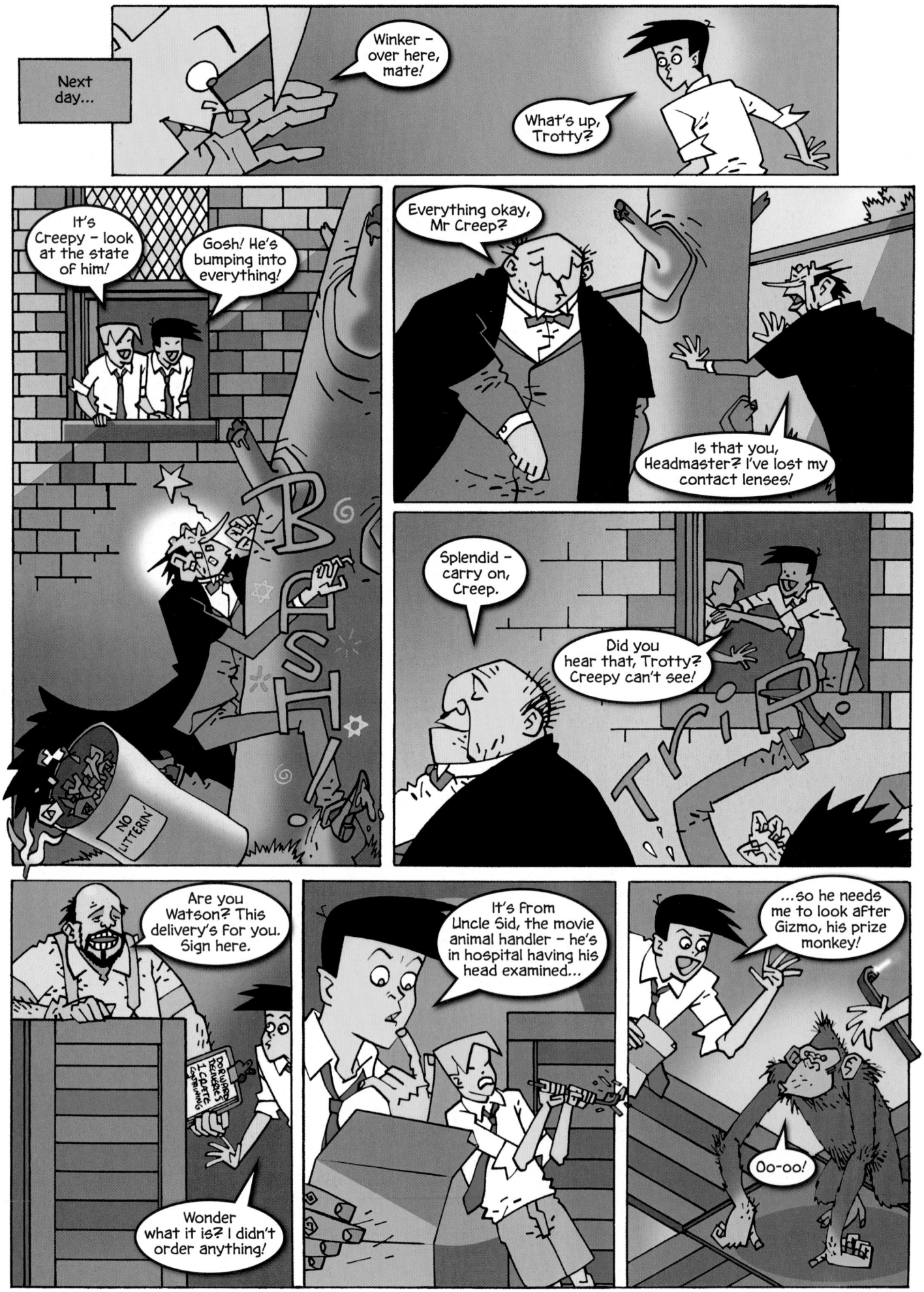
Next day...
Winker – over here, mate!
What's up, Trotty?
It's Creepy – look at the state of him!
Gosh! He's bumping into everything!
BASH!
NO LITTERIN'
Everything okay, Mr Creep?
Is that you, Headmaster? I've lost my contact lenses!
Splendid – carry on, Creep.
Did you hear that, Trotty? Creepy can't see!
TRIP.
Are you Watson? This delivery's for you. Sign here.
Wonder what it is? I didn't order anything!
It's from Uncle Sid, the movie animal handler – he's in hospital having his head examined...
...so he needs me to look after Gizmo, his prize monkey!
Oo-oo!

It says he's highly trained!
Let's see! Can you switch on my PSP, Gizmo.
Switch it on? He's only beaten your high score – that's all, Trotty!
Okay – he's bright, but how are you going to keep him hidden?
Creepy's so short-sighted now, all we'll need is a spare uniform.
There – a perfect disguise!
English test in five minutes – move yourselves!
Yes, Sir, Mr Creep!
Hmm! You could do with a haircut, boy!
Good! Creepy fell for the disguise!

And, while you're at it, you need a shave as well!
Rasp!
TOSS!
SKID!
Good shot, Gizmo.
CRASH!
YELP!
Careful, Sir. The janitor must have shined the floor for the inspectors today.
Ouch! Ow! You're right, Watson – to class, before anything else happens.
These sums need cleaned off the board – get dusting, boy.
snidey
creepy
Head
tut! tut tut!
So...
That's it – plenty elbow grease!
RUB
Plenty chalk dust – and Creepy's covered in it! Snigger!
That'll do, boy!

Lunchtime...
I've never seen the place looking so clean – even the cobwebs are polished!
If we don't watch out, we'll win that contest!
And the month at Swot Camp!
Wait! I've got the perfect wangle! Go to it, Gizmo!
Scamper!
Shortly...
Awesome – I've never seen such a mess!
School Of The Year Contest? No chance!
Meanwhile...
Parcel for you, Mr Creep.
Ah – my replacement contact lenses!
And these are from the optician's new range...
...TEACHER VISION! I can see!

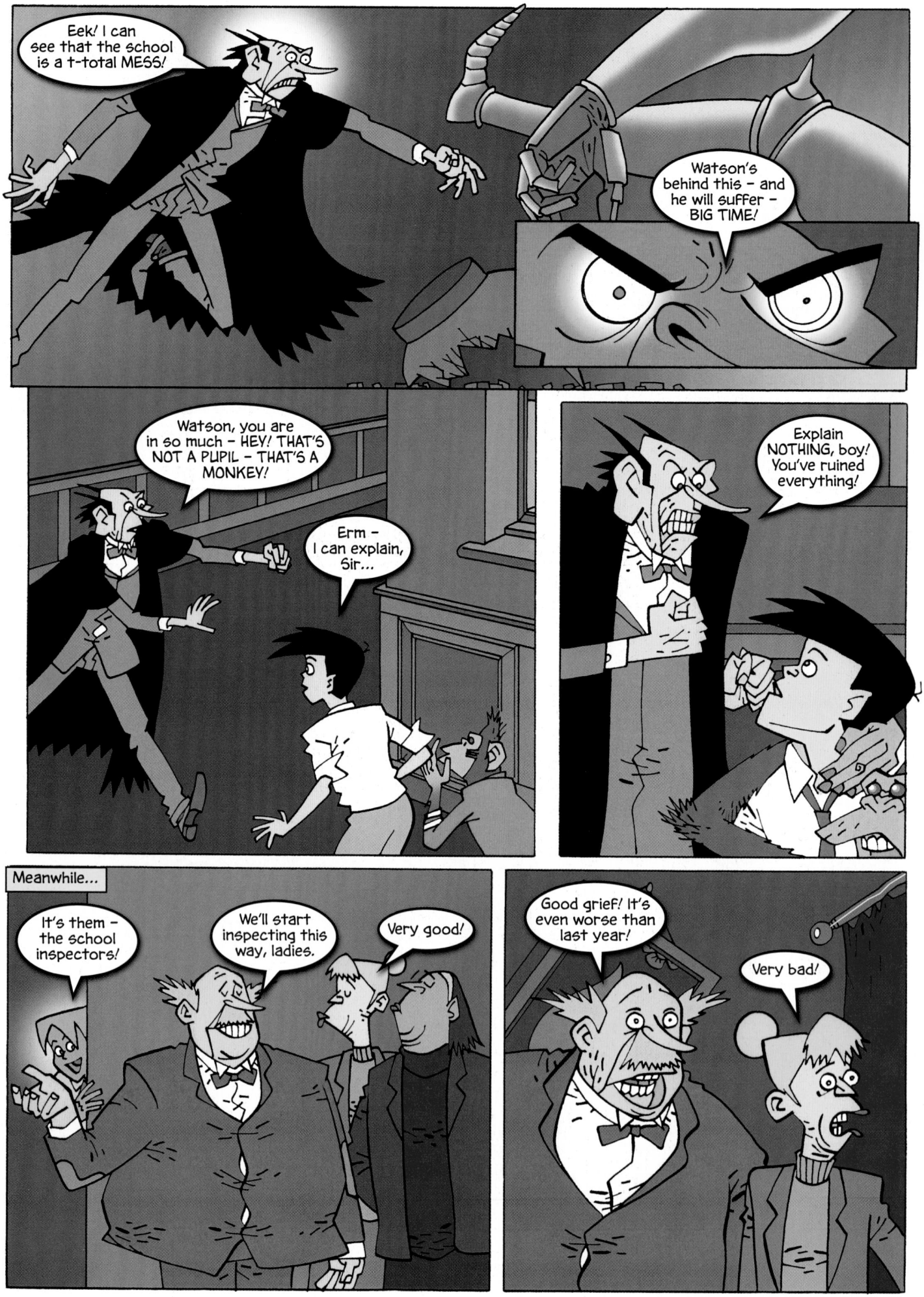
Eek! I can see that the school is a t-total MESS!
Watson's behind this - and he will suffer - BIG TIME!
Watson, you are in so much - HEY! THAT'S NOT A PUPIL - THAT'S A MONKEY!
Erm - I can explain, Sir...
Explain NOTHING, boy! You've ruined everything!
Meanwhile...
It's them - the school inspectors!
We'll start inspecting this way, ladies.
Very good!
Good grief! It's even worse than last year!
Very bad!

And don't try to hide, you buffoon of a baboon...
...you smelly, beastly, hairy, horrid...
You there! Creep, I'm talking to you! How dare you treat that pupil like an animal?
Crikey! The inspectors!
But, your inspectornesses, I w-was shouting at the m-monkey!
Monkey? MONKEY? Liar, liar - pants on fire! There's no monkey here!
Eh? But just a second ago...
Tee-hee! Gizmo's done a runner through the window!

This isn't the Dark Ages, Creep! Pupils must be treated with kindness and respect!
To make it up to them, we're sending them on a week's break to Disneyland...
...and YOU'LL be paying for it – out of your wages!
Whine!
Reee-sult!
So...
...so I left Gizmo at Greytowers as a playmate for him!
This is wicked, Winker – but what happened to Gizmo?
Well, I thought Creepy would be lonely all by himself...
Erk! Eek! Do y-you know, there ARE t-times when I don't really like Watson!
STREF'

WILLIAM THE CONKEROR MEERKAT

Puss and Boots
Aw, cool! It's Puss and Boots! These guys are great! They're always knocking the stuffing out of each other...
Lets just watch...
Any second now, it's all going to kick off...
Aw, come on!!!
CLANG!
Oh dear, what happened to you?
Duh?
Someone hit me with a frying pan!
You!
You have a frying pan behind your back!!!
That's just a coincidence. It could have been anyone.
GRRR! How come I've just logged onto your Twitter account, and it says "Just hit Puss with a frying pan! LOL!"

Erm, well... what you're forgetting is... erm...
CLANG!
This!
HA HA HA! This is me, running away!
HA HA HA
Nigel Auchterlounie
I'm gonna hide out here, in the park, until he calms down over that one!
HA, HA HA!
I'm still laughing about it now!
Oh, hold...on what's this? I've got a text.
"Behind H."
Uh oh.
CLANG!

JAK AND TODD
Snore-snort!
Beep-beep! Beep-beep! Beep-beep!
Jus' a few more minutes - where's the snooze button?
Zzz-snore-snurfle!
Jus' a few more minutes later...
Beep-beep! Beep-beep! Beep-beep!
Where's that...

...PESKY SNOOZE BUTTON?
BLAT!

Jus' a few more - zzzzzzzzzzzzzzzzzzz!

Later...
Yoohoo - it's 8.46am, Jak!
Eh? Stop joking, Mandy! You're joking - right?

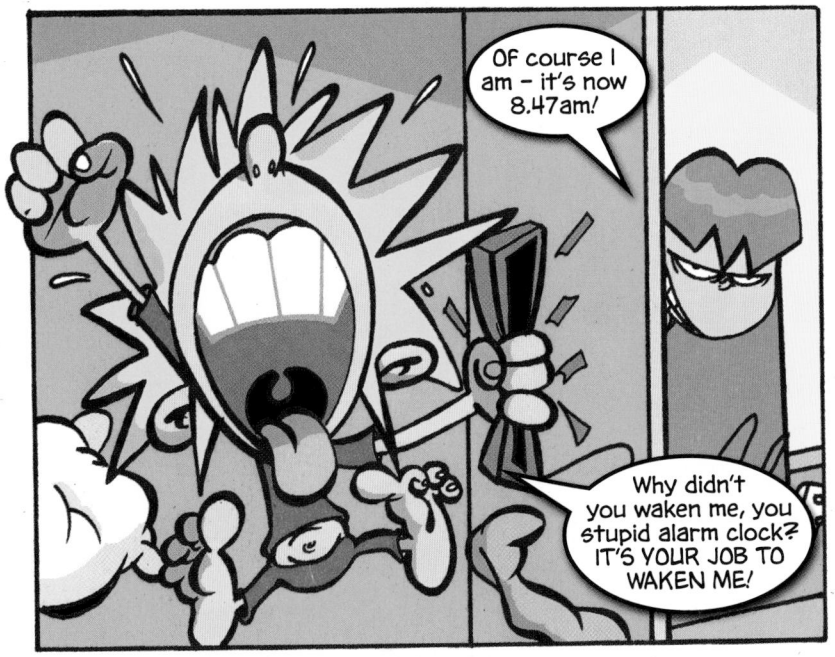
Of course I am - it's now 8.47am!
Why didn't you waken me, you stupid alarm clock? IT'S YOUR JOB TO WAKEN ME!

I may not be TOO late for school - at least the bathroom's free

It will be free – after I've finished! After me, you'll be first!
M-Mandy? NO-O-O-O!

Let me in! LET ME IN!
THUD!
Nope! Snigger!

Doomed! Mandy takes forever to disguise all the zits and plaster over the cracks!

I HEARD THAT!
Too easy! She fell for it – the oldest trick in the book!

Later...
Puff-pant! Hi, Todd – did you sleep in?
Pant-puff! Yep – you too?

Meet Mr Brisket...
10.44am – this is the latest Jak and Todd have ever been! I've got them bang to rights! Cackle! They're going to think they LIVE in the detention room!

Got the foreign coin?
Sure have - and you've got the sheet of paper, haven't you?
Aha! That sounded like a coin of the realm! Well, whatever it is, it's mine! After all...
TINKLE!
...finders keepers - ERK! That s-sounded like...
RIP!
...my pants - I ripped my pants - but where's the tear?
And in we sneak!
Yep - Brisket would have to get up REALLY early to catch US napping!

BRAIN DUANE
Wahey, a real work of art! Cracking likeness!
Hur hur, you'll be a work of art in a minute, big bonce!
BOOT
SPLOT
I think my effort is a much better likeness, yuk yuk!
FLUMP
Ornamental Snow Men are so last year. Now inflatable tinsel is all the rage!
STINKY RUBBISH TIP
Hmmm, time to get inventive, methinks!
STEVE BECKETT
CLANK
DUANE'S LAB
CLATTER
This is a work of sheer cunning!

Let's get you into position, my frosty friend! Chortle.
ZOOM
That goon just asks for trouble. Hur hur!
Yeeeeowwll!!
What's the matter Mack? You're looking a bit peaky...
CLANK
Are you sure you're getting your five-a-day? Maybe these will help - yuk yuk!
THONK
Aaaarrgh, mummy!
BONK
BZZTTTZZ
THONK
Yeeaargh! Abort mission! Abort!
Waaarrgglle!
KABOOOM
This will make you feel better, Duane. A nice drop of carrot soup!
Groan! Thanks, Mum!

BULLY BEEF and CHIPS
I got a magic kit for my birthday.
I know magic, too. Pick a hand.
Aha! Is something hidden in one of them?
Nope!
Oofyah!
Here's another good trick. I'll make something disappear.
Oh yeah? What?
Your face.
I know a better trick.
?
Tum-ti-tum.
Now that's magic!
Eep!

STRANGE HILL SCHOOL

Our stretch limo takes us to our posh school, scruffian.
Waiting for your old bus, peasant?
No – a coach, actually.

Haw-haw! A peasant with a sense of humour! A coach? Don't you mean a dustcart?
Snicker! Dustcart! Jolly good joke, Tarquin!
No – a coach – here it comes now!

?
Squeal!
What? No more jolly good jokes? Hmm? No?

Soon...
Getting the better of posh twits like them almost makes me enjoy being at Strange Hill School!
Almost – but not quite! LET GO! THAT'S THE ONLY ARM I'VE GOT ON THAT SIDE!
RIP!
Phew! Ta, Wolfie – that's the second time this week!
The janitor must have forgotten to feed it again!
You'll be late, boys!
Yeah, yeah! Whatever! Look at the state of my blazer, Wolfie.
Your mum isn't going to be best pleased, Eddie!
Grr! I'm not best pleased, either! Now snap to it! Snappitty-snap!
Yikes! The Head's bite is much worse than his bark! RUN!
Huh! You just beat me to class – by a short head – cackle!
Ow! Ouch! N-Not funny, Wolfie!
CHOMP!

It's Assembly First this morning, boys!
Aw, we had Assembly yesterday, Teacher.

Yes – well, Frankie wondered what would happen if he loosened his belly button...
Not again – he did that yesterday as well!

The game's afoot! Hee-hee!
Anyone need a hand?
Who knows where the nose goes?

Soon...
I'm not laughing – because this isn't funny – does anyone see me laughing?

Soon again...
Stay still – you don't want to lose your head again.
That's better!

Right! Your first real lesson today is Al...
What? Algebra? Wow! I don't believe it – a normal lesson!

Not Algebra – whatever that is – ALCHEMY!
What's Alchemy?
THIS is Alchemy, young Potter!
Oh, I get it...
NO! DON'T MIX...
...Alchemy's a bit like Chemistry...
KABOOOM!
...only m-more n-noisy!
?
Okay, Class – next l-lesson is FIND THE SCHOOL!

HISTORICAL MEERKATS
MARIE ANTOINETTE MEERKAT
XXL WIGS
SCHLICK
TA-DAA!

CORPORAL CLOTT

It looks like Corporal Clott should lose a little weight...
Grrr! Got to tell him to blinkin' do everything... mutter... grumble...
CREEK!
Crash!
Later, at 14,500 feet...
Right!
Parachute!
Go!
Go!
Go!
Corporal Clott! JUMP!!!
Oops!
Sir! Yes, sir!!!
Bah! That boy's so stupid, I have to tell him to do everything!
Now fall to Earth!

DESPERATE DAN
U.S.A. TOUR
PART 2
Want a lift, Dude?
You bet - are you going..?
I'm gone, Dude!
VROOOM!
Hey! I wasn't in yet! I've pulled your door off!
Still, this will be handy - if it gets too hot I can wind down the window!
Then...
Couldn't give me a lift, could you?
I certainly could!
H.H.
He wasn't joking - now this is what I call a lift!

Later...
REDWOOD NATIONAL PARK
Well, here I am in California – this place is first on my sight-seeing list!
Where are they?
BUMP!
Hey!
Now THIS could be what I'm looking for.
That's it! Wow! These Giant Redwoods sure are tall – and I think the pesky Redwood pollen is giving me hay fever!
AHCH
Yep! Sniff!
OOO!

Long - not tall - now the Giant Redwoods are long - since I sneezed! I guess this is what folks call "The Fall"!

It's time I was long - long gone from here!

Miles later...
I've just got to see THAT!
GRAND CANYON
AS A CANYON, IT'S GRAND!

Wow! It's Desperate Dan - would you like a tour of the Grand Canyon, Dan?
SEE THE GRAND CANYON BY AIR!
Sure would, pal!

This is a real honour to take you for a spin - I'm a great fan of yours, Dan!
Speaking of fans...

...do you mind if I turn this one off? The draught's ruffling my moustache!

The f-f-fan stopped okay, b-but now the helicopter's spinning!
HIRRR
Groan! That's the f-first time I've ever b-been airsick without leaving the g-ground!
Whoa, head! I didn't like that spin – I'll take some other kind of tour!
Yes! This is more like it – I'm at home in the saddle!
MULE TOUR TO CANYON FLOOR
SQUIDGE!
Drat! I'm a tad heavy for THIS saddle though!
M-My m-mule – SUNK!

So the mule tour's out - and there don't seem to be any other tours - drat!
There is one tour left, Dan - the Ten Second Tour!

The Ten Second Tour?
Yep - and it doesn't cost a cent - step thataway!

WHEEEEEEEEEEEEEEEEEE
Yikes!

PLOP!

Some time later...
I actually quite enjoyed the Ten Second Tour of the Grand Canyon, but I do have one itchy complaint...

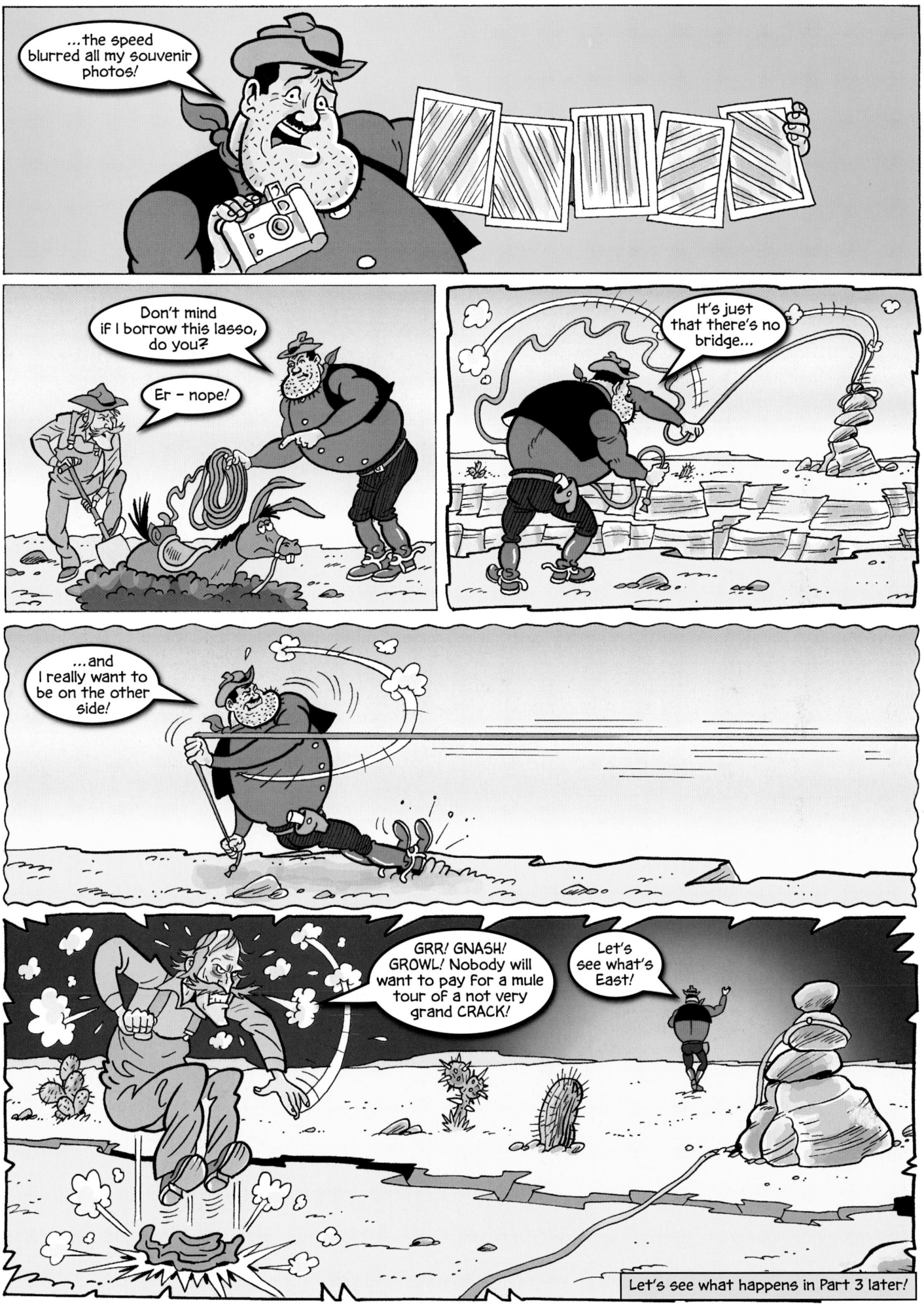
...the speed blurred all my souvenir photos!
Don't mind if I borrow this lasso, do you?
Er – nope!
It's just that there's no bridge...
...and I really want to be on the other side!
GRR! GNASH! GROWL! Nobody will want to pay for a mule tour of a not very grand CRACK!
Let's see what's East!
Let's see what happens in Part 3 later!

KID COPS
SCHOOL
DINING HALL
Dinner time at last! I wonder what's on the menu?
I heard there's a new dinner lady!
Er, what's the grey food?
Fish pie and mash.
Ew! Anything else?
HOT SLOP
Quiche and salad.
Yum! I'll have that!
But that's the same - just cold!
COLD SLOP
Cold mash counts as salad.
Kid Cops - get over here. Someone's passing duff grub!
KID COPS
On our way, Grassy Noel!
DAD'S SHED
COP SHOP
Hey! You're under arrest, lady!
SCHOOL DINING HALL
Enter at your own risk
Police
You'll never take me!
She's doing a runner!
BEANS
TINNED SPROUTS
LARD FLAKES

This tin of RUNNER BEANS will get her PULSES racing!
BOWL!
BEANS

Eek! No! Not the pot cupboard!
POTS + PANS — PLEASE DO NOT CRASH INTO.
ROLL!

CRASH!
CLATTER!
RATTLE! CLANG!
...and so on...

Will you come quietly?
Sniff. I would if I could...
sausage handcuffs
CLATTER!
CLANG!

Anyway, you're not real police! You can't do anything to me!

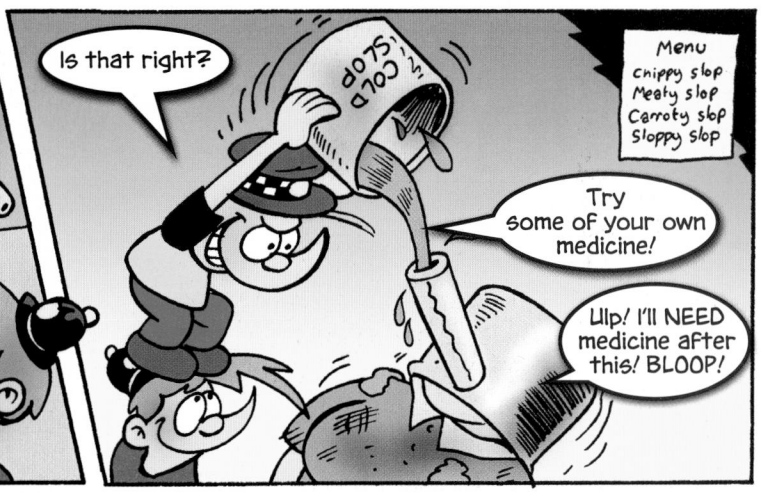
Is that right?
COLD SLOP
Menu
Chippy slop
Meaty slop
Carroty slop
Sloppy slop
Try some of your own medicine!
Ulp! I'll NEED medicine after this! BLOOP!

Later...
How's the grub now, Noel?
KID COPS

I would tell you...
...but it's rude to talk with your mouth full!
Menu: Posh Nosh cooked to perfection
Seconds, please!

Beryl the Peril
TO THE BEACH
Dad wanted a rest, so he brought me to the beach!

I'm off to catch some fish, Dad!

Peace, perfect peace...

Hey, Dad! I caught something!

Aw, he only wants to play with you! Isn't he cute?
GET THAT THING AWAY FROM ME!

Go away! Go play in the rockpools or something!

That should keep her out of trouble for a little while.

Look what I found, Dad... oops!
SNIP
SNAP
SNAP
SNIP
SNIP
SNAP

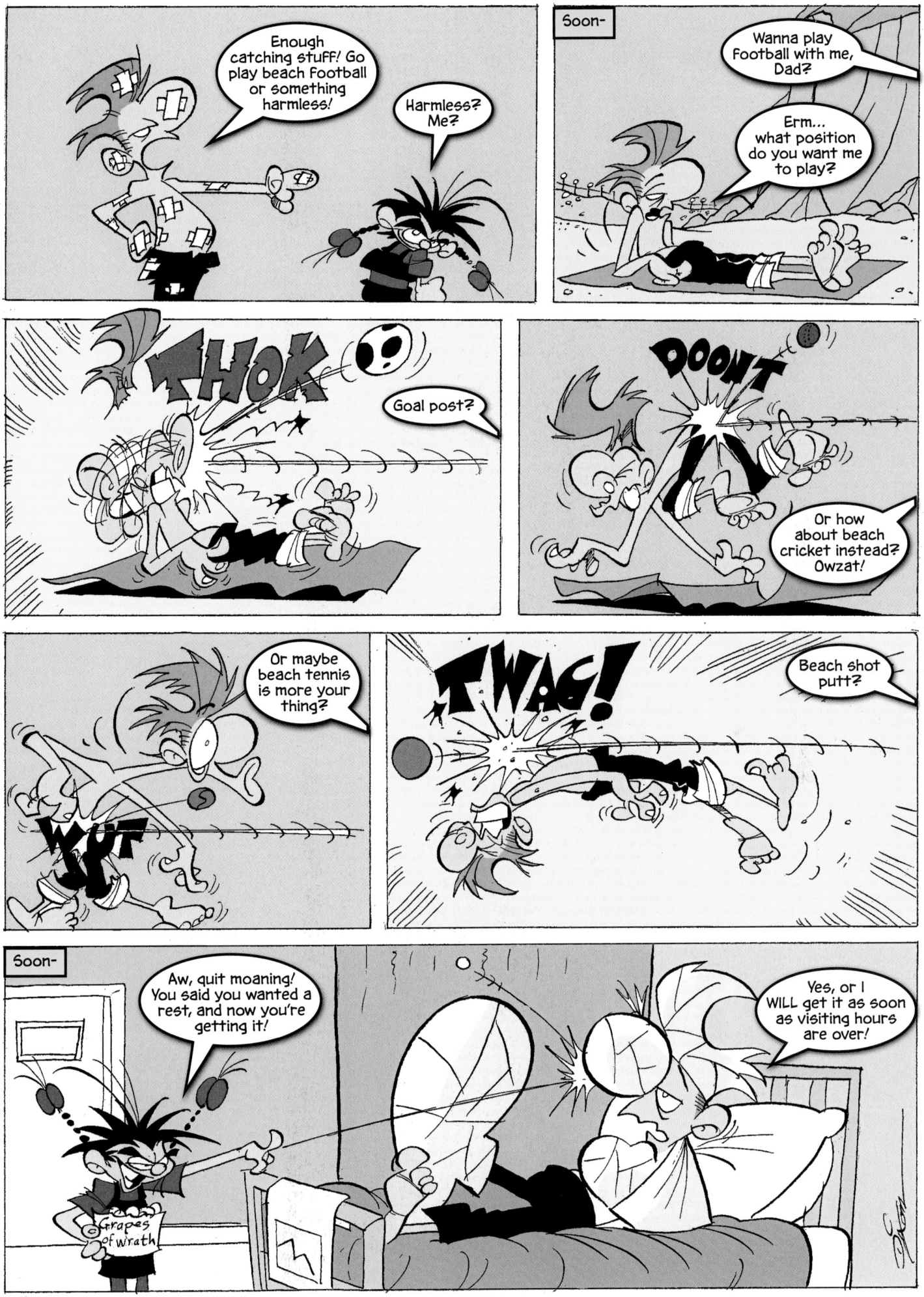
Enough catching stuff! Go play beach football or something harmless!
Harmless? Me?
Soon-
Wanna play football with me, Dad?
Erm... what position do you want me to play?
THOK
Goal post?
DOONT
Or how about beach cricket instead? Owzat!
Or maybe beach tennis is more your thing?
WUT
TWAG!
Beach shot putt?
Soon-
Aw, quit moaning! You said you wanted a rest, and now you're getting it!
Yes, or I WILL get it as soon as visiting hours are over!
Grapes of Wrath

BRAINEIEK

You're probably wondering what Charlie's thinking about – I'm thinking it too!

CLICK!
I've got it! What a great idea!
Woohoo! Charlie had an idea! All by himself!
CLANG-A-LANG!
HOP!

What is it? You don't look like you just had an idea...
Aw, it's too hard. I'd need nails and planks and stuff.

SLAP!
Leave it to me, Charlie-boy!
A problem shared is a problem doubled... or whatever that silly saying is.
CRUMP!

TWEET!
TWEET!
Did I get knocked over by a bus?
What's that noise?
Will you birds be quiet?!!

People say I have a magnetic personality.
And I do – I'll just switch it on.

Come on... come on...
Here we are! Nails! And lots of them!
CHUNG-A-CHING!
CHING! CHING!
Now for the planks.
Cow-a-bunga!
LEAP!
CHOPPITY-CHOP!
CHARLIE! We've got all the planks and nails you could ever want now!

Great! Now we can build my great idea – a treehouse!
Oh! A treehouse? That's... hmm... a problem.

Where did the tree go? You can't have a treehouse without a tree!

Now I'm worried about where you got the nails. Tell me where you got them!
Do I have to?

Phew! I don't have to, because you'll be able to work it out for yourself when you turn round!

Who'd have thought a house was held together with nails? How weird is that?
The house! You've destroyed the house, Brassneck! I'll get no pocket money for a zillion years!
CHOMP! CHOMP!

Hang on! I've got a new great idea!

So I rebuild the tree and then the house?
Right! And make it good, or I'll UNBUILD you!
NICK BRENNAN

Ollie Fliptrik
Woo-hoo! What a buzz!
Watch it, Ollie – you're grabbing too much air!
KRAK
Told you!

Oh, man! I've broken another deck!
That's the third this month!
Your mum is so going to kill you!

Nah! No problem! Watch this – I'll just turn on the old Ollie charm!

WHAAAT
So much for the old Ollie charm!

...and what's more, you're staying in until you learn to stop breaking expensive things!
Yeah, yeah! And what am I supposed to do in here all day? It's boring!

But my virtual reality skate game isn't – I could play with that!
VIRTUAL SK8ER

Soon...
There! That's me all wired up and ready to go!

Man, this virtual reality thing is sweet...

...I can grind...

...jump...

...do 360s...

...in fact, it feels just like the real thing - GNARLY!

WHAT? WHAT THE..? WHAT HAVE YOU DONE TO MY LOVELY FURNITURE?
Oops! I think my virtual reality game turned into TOTAL reality!

AAAAA
I think Ollie's mum has lost it - big time!

So...
So how come your mum bought you a new deck?
Yeah - and let you out?
She said it was cheaper to replace my deck than the whole house - PARTY!

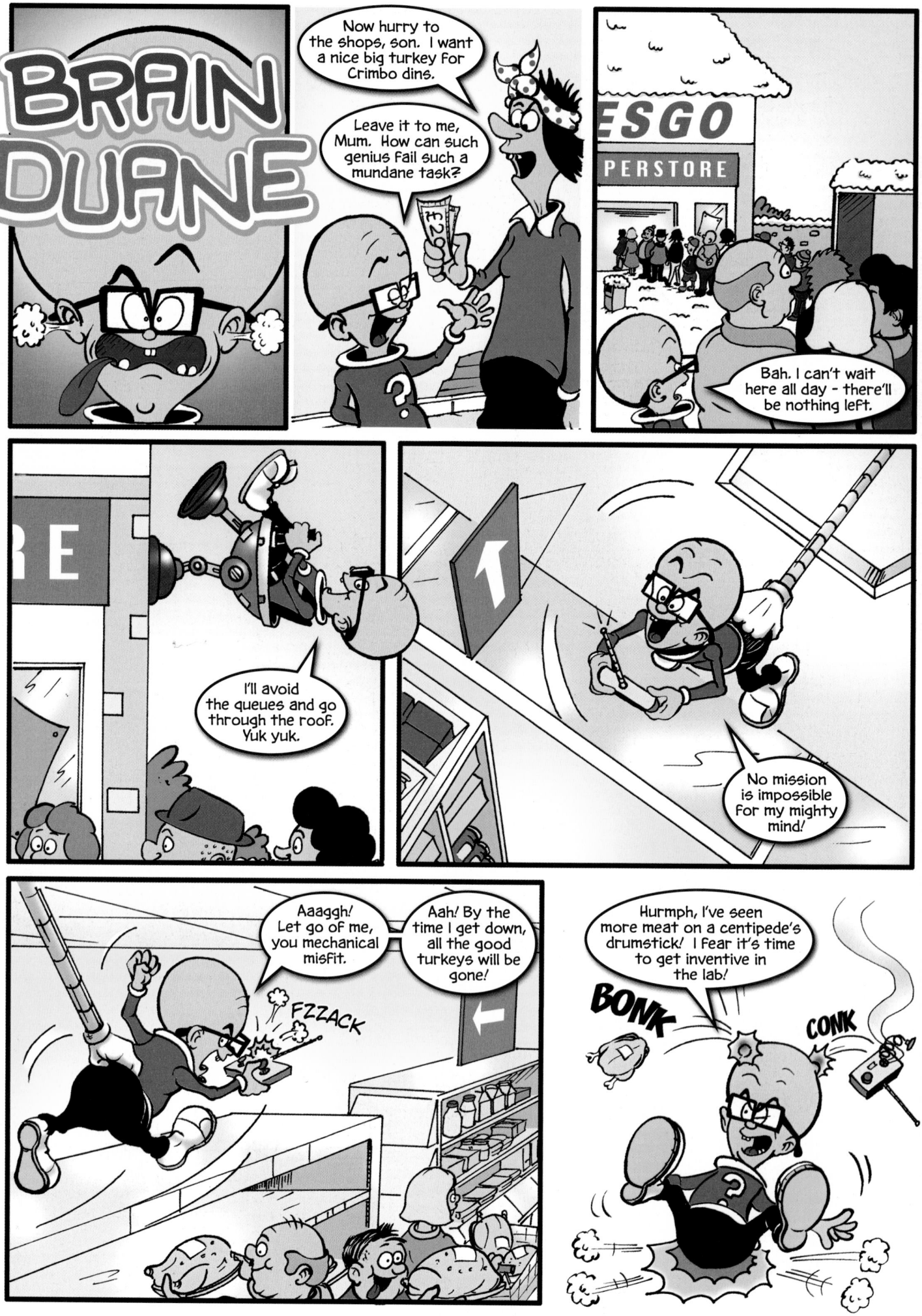
BRAIN DUANE
Now hurry to the shops, son. I want a nice big turkey for Crimbo dins.
Leave it to me, Mum. How can such genius fail such a mundane task?
£20
ESGO
PERSTORE
Bah. I can't wait here all day - there'll be nothing left.
I'll avoid the queues and go through the roof. Yuk yuk.
No mission is impossible for my mighty mind!
Aaaggh! Let go of me, you mechanical misfit.
Aah! By the time I get down, all the good turkeys will be gone!
FZZACK
Hurmph, I've seen more meat on a centipede's drumstick! I fear it's time to get inventive in the lab!
BONK
CONK

DUANE'S LAB
KERACKLE
CLANK
POP
I saw this in a comic once. Let's see if it really works. Chortle.
Wahey, here goes! I bet Gordon Ramsay wishes he had one of these.
Just switch this to the desired setting.
SMALL
AVERAGE
BIG
MASSIVE
TITCHY
CLICK
Duane, where's my blinking turkey?
BZZZTTTZZZ
It's coming, Mum... just another second... titter.
Here you go, Mum. Is this big enough?.. (cough) eh hem.. Merry Christmas!
SMASH
CRUNNCH!!
SHRIEK!! You brainstorming buffoon, come down 'ere! I'll give you a Merry Christmas... Grrrr!
STEVE BECKETT

HISTORICAL MEERKATS
FLORENCE NIGHTINGALE
the meerkat with the lamp
KA-BOOM!
HOSPITAL
AMMUNITION AND EXPLOSIVE DUMP

BANANAMAN
Bananaskills
It's me again – Eric. Those of you who have been paying attention will know that I turn into Bananaman when I eat a banana.
For those of you who HAVEN'T been paying attention, here is a repeat.
MUNCH! GUZZLE!
There – and here is another repeat...
...BURRRRRRP! Beg pardon – sorry about that!
Now let me take you back in time and show you how I mastered my Bananaskills! Doo-eeee-eee-oooooooo!
Reader's voice
So creepy singing ISN'T one of your Bananaskills then?

Okay – no more singing! Back in time we go!
I look like a superhero – I wonder how strong I am?

Erk! Stronger than the mirror I hope – maybe I shouldn't have smiled at it!
CRASH!

Here's another "maybe" – maybe I can FLY!

CRUMP!

Okay – maybe I can fly OUTdoors!

Right – now how do I do this? UP, UP AND AWAYYYYYY!

FLAP!
FLAP!
FLAP!
FLAP!
FLAP!
FLAP!
Nope! How about this? TO INFIRMARY AND BEYOND!

Not that either! I bet if I got a start I could fly though!
Well, THAT horn gave me a start for a start!
BEEP!
Hey! What d'you know? I'm flying!
WHUMP!
Okay – so I'm not actually steering, but I am flying!
I'm learning though! Look! I'm learning to actually fly upwards and I'm learning...

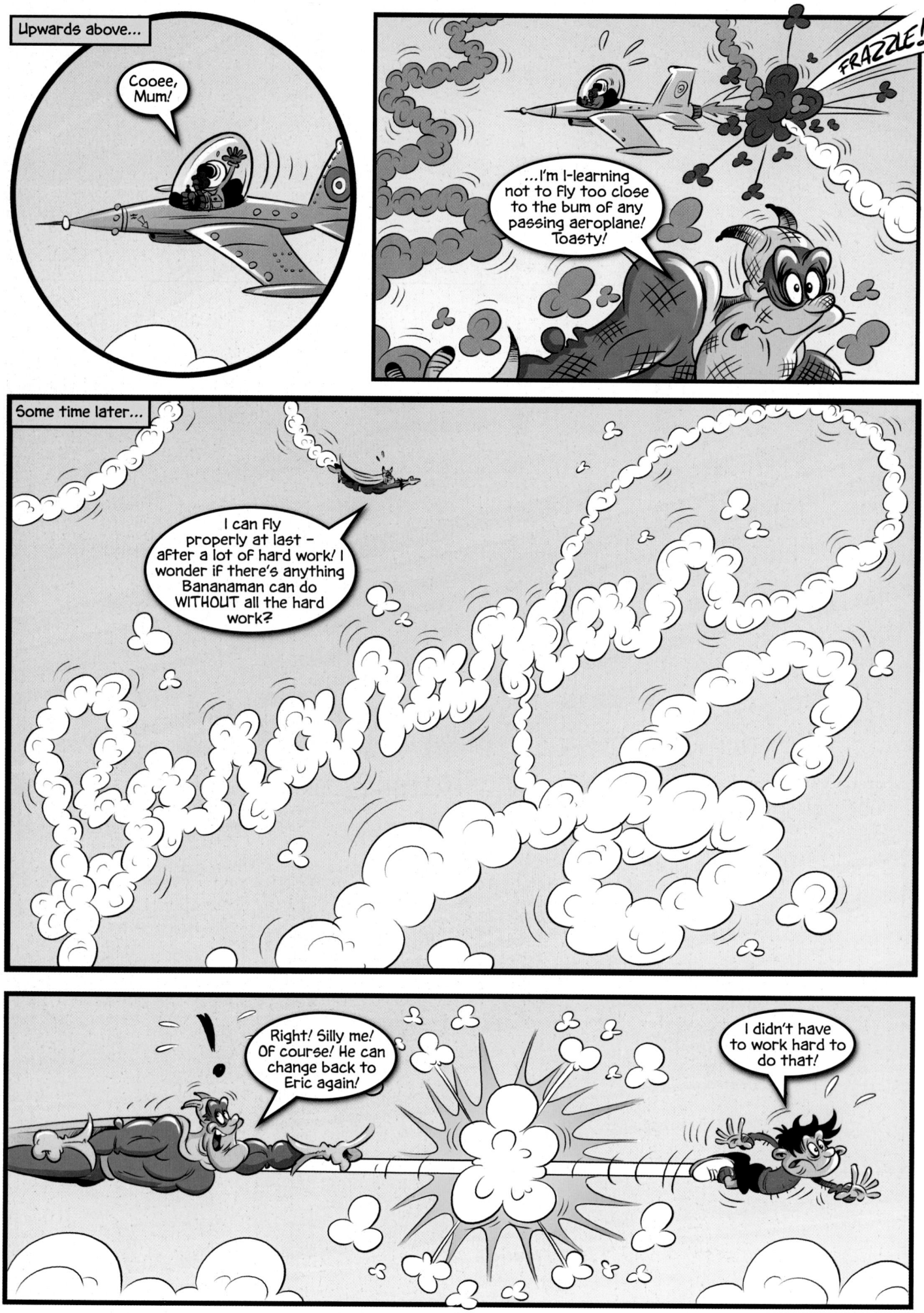
Upwards above...
Cooee, Mum!
FRAZZLE!
...I'm l-learning not to fly too close to the bum of any passing aeroplane! Toasty!
Some time later...
I can fly properly at last – after a lot of hard work! I wonder if there's anything Bananaman can do WITHOUT all the hard work?
!
Right! Silly me! Of course! He can change back to Eric again!
I didn't have to work hard to do that!

And this high-speed plummet – I can do this – this isn't hard either!
CRUMP!
Okay – now THAT was hard! Whimper!
Right, all you readers out there in readerland – gather all your things together – we're going back, BACK to the future – er – present – whenever!
– CHRIS McCHIE –
There is one thing Bananaman could never do, readers...
...and that's erase painful memories – that landing HURT! Poor Eric couldn't sit down for weeks!

Fiddle O'Diddle
BOOM!
Muldoon! What in t'blazes are ye up to?
I've come for ye gold, Fiddle! Just get back to bed.
Can ye not come back in t' morning, Muldoon? I be needing me sleep!
No chance, O'Diddle! I've realised where you've hidden t' gold and I'm not letting ye move it!
It's up ye tree, and I'm blasting it out!
Really?

Would it not be a good idea to get up there and have a look yerself?
Hmm, 'tis a fair point. Do you have a ladder?
I've a better idea, sit yerself in that there cannon, Muldoon.
Get me right there at the top.
Of course!
Hang on, I'm in a cannon!
Wait! I've changed my m
BOOM!
Mammy!!
Would ye look at that, there's me house!
CRASH!
MULDOON TOWERS (keep out)

Puss and Boots
CLEAN
PEEL
CLEAN
Grrr! It's that cheeky cat!
I'm gonna bosh him!
CRASH!
Oof!
RUN
HA! HA! HA! HA! HA! HA! HA!
Boots plans his revenge...
Puss steps on the pressure pad, which trips the anvil...
...then the shark moves in...
PUSS
RIP
...but on E-Bark, the one stop shop for revenge planning dogs, the price of sharks and anvils is way too expensive.
Especially for a dog with no job!
E-BARK

So...
Puss, the thing with the patio doors really had me miffed. So this was going to be my revenge... but I can't afford it.
Wow! This is really something! All this for me? It's a bit much for my window trick, isn't it?
PUSS
RIP

I know!
SLAM!

This is cheaper!
Jump!
Jump!
Jump!
Jump!
Jump!

Later...
Humm, maybe we need to break this endless cycle of violence. I get revenge on him. He gets revenge on me, so I get revenge back...

This is no way to live. I should be thinking about settling down. I'm too old for this. I am nearly seven now!

Trouble is, this is so much fun!
Z Z Z Z Z Z
Nigel Auchterlounie

WAKE UP!
Yikes!
LEAP!

HA HA HA! Look at him dance!

Beryl the Peril
Come on, Beryl. We're going to the museum today.
And I remembered the prod, so behave.
CATTLE PROD
But I'm allergic to boredom, Dad.

It'll be fun! We'll start with the Natural History Museum and then move on to...
You mean there's MORE THAN ONE museum?

These Spheniscus Penguins are really fascinating!
Boorrrr...

...ing! Hey, is that a dinosaur?
No dinosaurs today. Remember the last time!
I'm STILL the only living man with a Diplodocus bite scar!
SPHENISCUS PENGUINS

Soon-
WELCOME TO THE SCIENCE MUSEUM
Natural History Museum
There! Wasn't that educational?
Yeah, I learnt not to waste my life in museums!

Please don't take me into another museum! I can't take it! I CAN'T TAKE IT!
Oh, behave! This is the Science Mus...

...and welcome to our lecture on animatronics, the science of making things seem alive with the use of a remote control!
Huh?

And...
It's working! My little girl is learning! Everything's going to be okay!

Okay, I learnt enough!
She's been gone a while now. What's she up to?
That sounds like her now... oh, dear.
You were right, Dad! Museums can be fun! Giddyup, Rex!
Run!
Save yourselves!
Dixon

CUDDLES & DIMPLES
Suppertime! It's your favourite, boys – spaghetti!
NIGEL PARKINSON
There's one thing about our boys.
They're not greedy – they don't mind sharing.
That's why they're not fat – they don't actually eat a lot!
Guzzle!
They splash it everywhere else!
Slurp!
Finished, are we?
Yep – burp!
That was ace!

Good! In that case, it's bath...
GIRLY PONG SHAMPOO
...time! DAD! THEY'VE DONE A RUNNER AGAIN!
No worries! I've got them!
OUR LOVELY BOYS
Actually, no! THEY would appear to have got ME!
THUMP!
OOYAH!
GRANDAD
You may have escaped from your father...

...but there's no escape from me!
MUM
AGE 2
Missed, Mum!
Erk!
Aw, no! Missed again!
What an athlete - you should be on TV, Mum!
Okay - you should be on the floor then!
Do you think this is funny? I don't think this is funny!
SKID!
I'm - puff - gaining now though!
You are indeed, Mum!
MUM'S TV TIME: MUM CAN WATCH TV: ANY DAY ANY TIME EXCEPT DURING FOOTBALL SEASON SAT. 3-3.15
SATURDAY 3PM-3.15PM IS DADDY'S TV TIME (EXCEPT JUNE-MARCH)

So we're PULLING!
And I'm s-slipping! Oo-er!
Snigger! We don't have to tell you what she's doing now, do we?
CRASH!
High 5, Bro – we've had our fun and shown our parents who are the bosses!
Yep! We're ready for our bath now!
But...
A bath? Yeah – right! Mum's all hot and bothered from chasing you and I'm all bruised from hitting the floor hard! After Mum and me, you two will be first to have a bath!
Rats!
BATHROOM
SPLISH!
SPLASH!
SPLOSH!
Girly Bath in progress come back in 2 hours

AGENT DOG 2 ZERO

What's that? Yes... you're right. There is a fly in the ointment!
WHISPER! WHISPER!!
WAG! WAG!
Agent Dog 2 Zero, swotty dog and my rival to be Master's Number One Pet!
What we need is a plan to get rid of the botty-scratching bozo. But how..?
MASTER'S HOME!
I know it's winter, but I don't remember any avalanches happening round here before!
Agent Dog 2 Zero! I should have guessed!
Guess what Master brought home?
TUG! HEAVE!!

Here's a clue - it's the Christmas tree!
Ow! Gerroff!
Grr! I don't like being rubbed up the wrong way!
Look at him! What a goody-two-shoes!
Decorating the tree, Zero? Good boy!
Bah! What a swot!
Xmas decs
Still, I am the smartest pet in the house - fetch me a watering can, Cheese Burger!
RUB! RUB!!
A little while later-
I can't wait to see that fly in the ointment get his just desserts!

When Master sees the tree is wet, he'll think Zero has had a little tinkle!
Now I just sit back and watch the Fireworks!
Hmm... it looks good, but it's missing something.
AAAARRRRGGGGHHHH!!!
CLICK!
Cheese Burger! Forget the Fly, and bring me the ointment!
Of course - well done, Tiddles! Every Christmas tree needs a FURRY at the top!

Ollie Fliptrik
Groan! It feels like the snow's been here forever!
I know - we haven't been able to skate for over two weeks!

Hello, losers!
Get lost, Blanchet!
DOG BOY

Hey! What's that thing on the front of your bike, Billy?
It's exactly what it looks like - a snow plough!
DOG BOY

Cool! Could you run it round the skate park?
Yeah! You'd be doing us a great favour!

Let me see - me help you lot out? Erm...

...that would be a NO! Snigger!
Let me at him! I'll - I'll...
You'll chill, big guy! I've got a plan!

Soon...
My mobile - - it must be Mr Stevens, my boss!
RING!

BILLY, GET YOUR WORTHLESS BACKSIDE TO THE SKATE PARK AND PLOUGH IT CLEAR OF SNOW! I HEAR THERE'S A SKATE-OFF AND I WANT YOU TO SELL LOADS OF HOT DOGS! WELL? WHAT ARE YOU WAITING FOR? GET MOVING!
Coo, that was quite gentle - Mr Stevens must be in a good mood.

But I won't chance it - I'm moving, Mr Stevens!
Must get it cleared - puff-pant - or Mr Stevens will do something nasty to my wages!
SK8 PARK

So...
Hey! Thanks, Billy - most kind of you!
Gasp! Wheeze! I didn't do it for you - I did it for my boss, Mr Stevens!

That reminds me - have you ever heard my impersonation of your boss? BILLY, GET YOUR WORTHLESS BACKSIDE TO THE SKATE PARK AND PLOUGH IT CLEAR OF SNOW!

Well, what do you think, Billy? Just like Mr Stevens, wasn't it? Cackle!
I don't think we want to know what Billy's thinking right now! Chuckle!
Grr! Splutter! Mutter!

WINKER WATSON in Tuck In
Tut-tut! There are the boys going to squander all their pocket money in town again, Headmaster.

Aha! I've just had a brilliant idea to put all their pocket money in MY pocket!

Sorry, boys! The town's out of bounds in case you – er – come down with something nasty.
Aw, but we were going to the tuck shop, Mr Creep!

And you can still go to the tuck shop, boys!
Eh? Since when did Greytowers have a tuck shop?

Since now!
School Dining Hall
Tuck Shop
This is just the school dining hall!
And where's the tuck?

There!
School dinner leftovers?
We wouldn't eat them for dinner - what makes you think we'll buy them now?

Because THIS is the only tuck shop you've got, Watson!
Erk! He's right - we're banged-up!

Not for long though - I've thought up a wangle! Fetch the archery gear, Trotty.
Why? I don't get it!

To take it up to the clock tower of course!

So...
4
5
6
I still don't get it - why are you aiming for that tree?
Because that tree's outside the school and now we can make...

A zip slide for us to get out of school? Brilliant!
TWANG!
Not US, Trotty...

6
...THIS!
A dummy? I don't get it again!
Below...
That boy's attempting to break out of school!
Puff! Pant! I wager Watson's behind this escape attempt!
Creepy's right – I am behind this!
He won't escape that easily though!
I still don't get it, Winker – we're no nearer to getting to town!
Patience, Trotty!

Oh, dear! I'm too heavy! I'm dragging the zip slide down! I d-don't think I'm g-going to make it over...
...NO-OH-OH-OH-OUCH!
KER-UNCH!
I GET IT!
Snigger! So did Creepy! Boy, did he get it?
Going to town? Didn't Mr Creep lock the school gate?
Yes, but we don't need the key, Headmaster.
Not since Creepy came down with something nasty...
...THE SCHOOL WALL - RIGHT ON TOP OF HIM!
Come back, boys - the school tuck shop has delicious second day's cabbage - a bargain at only £1.50!

CORPORAL CLOTT
The radar system is a vital part of our nation's defences...
GRAAAA!!!
What is this!?! You, soldier! What are you doing!?!
Er... I'm watching the South East airspace, Colonel Grumbly. In case of an attack on London or Dover!
And...and...I'm watching the North, sir. F-For Russian spy planes!
And what about you, Corporal Clott!?!
I'm watching Ice Age 3. Because... erm, No. I got nothin'.
Come 'ere!!!
Yikes!
You can't be trusted with our nation's safety. So you're on tank painting duty. I'll be back in one hour, and that thing had better be green!!!
Sir! Yes, sir!
SLAP!
Ow, I hurt my face a bit when I did that salute.
1 hour later...
Corporal Clott's a complete idiot, so what I need to do is stick with jobs like this one. Jobs he can't get wrong.
What!!!
Phew! Just finished in time!
It's pink!!! Why's it pink!?! Pink!!! Why!?!
Something tells me it's not green, is it?

Ten minutes later...
Well, Doc?
He's completely colour-blind, Colonel Grumbly. All colours, to him, will look like shades of grey.
Grrrr!
If I didn't know better I'd say you were colour-blind on purpose!
Right then, Clott! Clean these explosive shells. You don't need colours for that!!!
Nigel Auchterlounie
Sir! Yes, sir!!!
ARRRRGH! What are you doing!?! You'll kill us all!!!
You said to hit it with hammers.
Well, Doc?
His ears were full of ear wax. Look at all this stuff!
No wonder he mis-heard you.
Mis-heard!?! "You don't need colours for that" doesn't sound at all like "Hit it with hammers"!!!
Well, he's also really stupid.
Right! well, I guess there's nothing to stop you cleaning those shells now Corporal Clott!
Sir! Yes, Sir!
Maybe he can hear now Colonel Grumbly, but that doesn't mean he's not still an idiot!

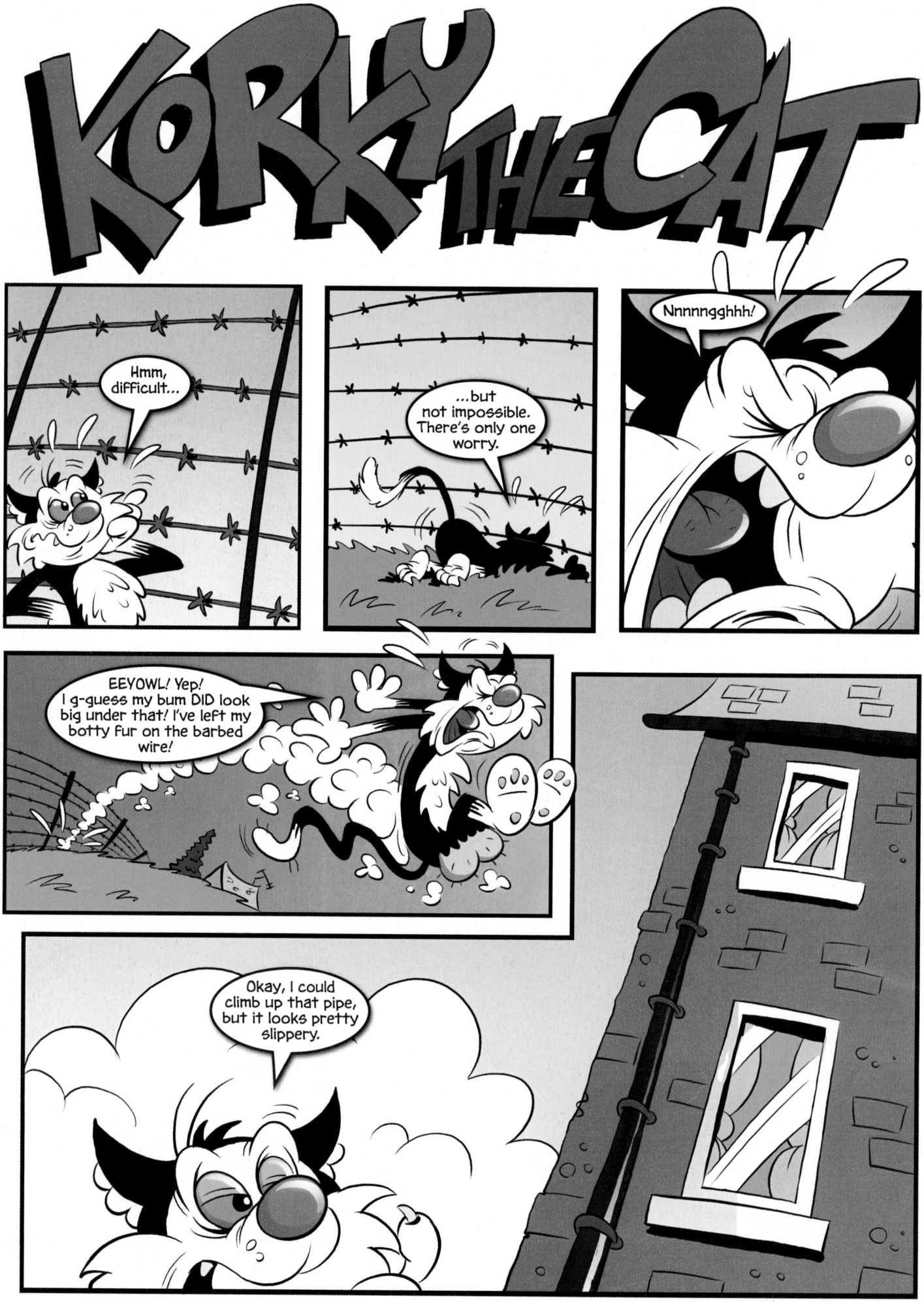
KORKY THE CAT
Hmm, difficult...
...but not impossible. There's only one worry.
Nnnnngghhh!
EEYOWL! Yep! I g-guess my bum DID look big under that! I've left my botty fur on the barbed wire!
Okay, I could climb up that pipe, but it looks pretty slippery.

Let's measure the pipe...
...and me. Yes, I'll fit – so...
...this way should be safer!
Made it! Now I need my favourite claw for this next bit!
SCHICK!
Eep! Sorry about that – sets your teeth on edge, doesn't it?
SKREEEK!
It's okay, Kits – it's just me!
Forgotten your door key, Uncle Korky?
Again?
That's the third time this week!

GEORGE VS DRAGON
PRESENTS
"BAYEUX TRAVESTY"
GEORGE WAS A BRAVE AND HANDSOME KNIGHT LOVED BY ALL OF THE LADIES.
ONE DAY GEORGE WAS CALLED UPON BY THE KING OF ENGLAND.
"I NEED YOUR HELP, GOOD KNIGHT" SAID THE KING.

"I NEED YOU TO DEFEAT AN EVIL DRAGON!" SAID THE KING
"I'LL DO IT!" SAID GEORGE, AND EVERYONE LET OUT A CHEER.
AND SO GEORGE HEROICALLY SET OFF ON HIS EPIC QUEST...
...UPON HIS MIGHTY STEED, SUSAN.
THEY CROSSED THE SEAS WITHOUT TROUBLE...
...BUT BRAVE GEORGE KNEW THAT GREAT DANGER LAY AHEAD...

AND SOON GEORGE FOUND THE DRAGON, WHO WAS GIANT AND FEROCIOUS AND BAD.
AND SMELLY, TOO.
THEN THE DRAGON ATTACKED POOR GEORGE
BUT GEORGE LEAPT FORTH AND...
WAITAMINUTE! That didn't happen! This tapestry is all LIES!
FANTON '11
And why does it end so suddenly?
I ran out of THREAD, okay?
Hmph. I'd like to see YOU make an awesome tapestry.
SULK!
YE END!

DESPERATE DAN IN U.S.A. TOUR PART 3
Are we nearly there yet? Are we nearly there yet? Are we nearly there yet?
No! No! And no!
One minute later-
How about now?
NO! NO! NO!
CLANG!
You're driving me to DISTRACTION!
What? But I want to get to BUFFALO!
I'm going to have a look up front.
Boo-hoo! That was my grandaddy's shovel!
I can't see any more from up here than I could back there!
Soon-
Cripes! I'm as black as a black cat in a coal cellar with no lights! I can't go sight-seeing like this!
BUFFALO NY

What I need is a shower – and this will do just nicely!
Howdy, officer! Now that I'm presentable again, can you direct me to them Niagara Falls?
I can – they're right behind you.
Wow! What a sight – but there's only one thing I want to see after a good wash...
And you just used them as a shower!
...one of Aunt Aggie's cow pies! I'm getting homesick!
Cactusville, here I come!
ZIP!

Aunt Aggie! I'm home!
Oh, Dan! I've been so worried! Where have you been?
I've been sightseeing all over the United States, but I just had to come home –
A HAPPY HOME IS A DESPERATE HOME
—Dan's Grandad
I missed your cow pies too much!
Oh? You missed my cow pies?
But you didn't miss ME enough to send one little postcard? Get out! Scram! Git!
Help! I know one thing for sure – the cow pies aren't missing me!

DANDY BOOK
EXIT
GET OUT!
Bobbly!
Wobbly!
BUM WAXING
Gerroff.
BLOB